STARDUST
Chronicles of Hollywood's Finest Era
MEMORIES

I0486755

"A mesmerizing journey back in time!"
Diane Robertson

"Felt like I was right there on the set with the stars."
Michael Vasquez

"A must-read for every film aficionado."
Liam Spencer

Robert Opnig

978-1-4467-6005-5
Imprint: Lulu.com

9 781446 760055

For all those who find magic in the flicker of old films, and for the legends of yesteryears who continue to inspire dreams, both on and off the screen.

FOREWORD

In the vast landscape of cinematic history, there remains a period so impactful, so transformative, that its glow can still be felt when we reminisce about the golden days of film. "Stardust Memories: Chronicles of Hollywood's Finest Era" by Robert Opnig is not just a tribute to that era, but a well-researched and passionately penned chronicle that encapsulates its magic.

Having known Robert for many years, his profound love and respect for classic cinema have always been evident. In this book, he has transcended from being a mere observer to a storyteller, narrating tales that were previously confined to dusty corners and forgotten reels. Through his words, the legends of the silver screen come to life once more, their stories echoing with the same charm, drama, and intrigue as they did in their prime.

As you delve into these pages, expect to be transported back in time. Robert paints Hollywood not just as a place but as a realm of dreams where everything was possible. It was an era of discovery, of innovation, and most significantly, of storytelling that remains unparalleled.

Reading "Stardust Memories" was for me a journey of rediscovery. Robert's narratives, rich in detail and sentiment, made me appreciate the nuances and intricacies of films and personalities that I thought I knew. The book serves both as an informative guide for those unfamiliar with Hollywood's Golden Age and a nostalgic trip for those who hold dear memories of it.

In a world of fleeting moments and ever-changing trends, it is essential to look back and appreciate the roots from which modern cinema has grown. "Stardust Memories: Chronicles of Hollywood's Finest Era" is more than just a testament to that bygone era; it is an invitation to experience its allure.

As you turn these pages, I hope you find the same joy, fascination, and admiration for Hollywood's finest era as I did.

Patrick Hendis

STARDUST MEMORIES: CHRONICLES OF HOLLYWOOD'S FINEST ERA

I n the sprawling expanse of Los Angeles, California, in the early 20th century, a relatively nondescript district began to gain prominence as the epicenter of a burgeoning new industry. The district's name? Hollywood. Though synonymous today with glamour, fame, and cinematic brilliance, Hollywood's beginnings were rather humble. Its transformation from a modest community into the world's film capital is a narrative rife with ambition, innovation, and serendipity.

At the turn of the century, New York City was the hub of American filmmaking. Its studios churned out films, but the chilly weather, lack of diverse landscapes, and patent wars led filmmakers to search for a new location. They found an idyllic haven on the west coast. Hollywood's abundant sunshine, varied topography, and distance from Thomas Edison's Motion Picture Patents Company in New Jersey made it a particularly appealing choice. Edison's company had a tight grip on the patents of film equipment, often leading to litigations against unlicensed filmmakers. Hollywood's remote location offered an escape from this constant legal scrutiny.

The first film made in Hollywood was a seventeen-minute short titled "In Old California" in 1910, directed by D.W. Griffith. The film's success was a beacon to other filmmakers, signaling the potential of Hollywood as a prime location for film production. As more filmmakers migrated west and started setting up studios, the district's reputation as a cinematic hub began to solidify. By the 1920s, Hollywood had indisputably become the heartland of American cinema.

The 1920s marked significant developments that would shape the film industry for decades to come. The introduction of sound, or "talkies" as they were colloquially known, was revolutionary. The first synchronized dialogue in a feature film was introduced in "The Jazz Singer" in 1927. Though not the first film to have synchronized sound, its commercial success marked the decline of silent films and set a new standard for movies.

During the same period, notable studios established their roots, including Paramount, Warner Bros., MGM, and Twentieth Century Fox. Each studio began carving out its niche, and stars like Charlie Chaplin, Buster Keaton, and Mary Pickford became household names. Their films weren't just viewed as entertainment but as artworks, establishing cinema as a vital component of cultural discourse.

However, Hollywood wasn't just about films. The district became symbolic of the American Dream. Actors, directors, writers, and producers flocked to Hollywood in search of opportunities, lured by stories of fame and fortune. The studios, well aware of this allure, began crafting the images of their stars meticulously, creating larger-than-life personas that the public eagerly devoured.

As the 1920s came to a close, the groundwork was firmly laid for Hollywood's Golden Age, an era that would see the industry reach unprecedented heights of creativity, influence, and prominence. With its unique blend of art, business, and spectacle, Hollywood was poised to captivate the world, and its journey had only just begun.

B efore the unmistakable cadence of spoken dialogue graced cinema screens, film narratives were driven by expressive visuals, exaggerated acting, and intertitles that conveyed snippets of dialogue or crucial plot points. The silent era wasn't merely a prelude to the talkies; it was a rich and innovative epoch of its own, laying foundational aesthetics and storytelling techniques for generations of filmmakers to come.

At the forefront of this era stood a pantheon of luminous figures, but none shone as brightly as Charlie Chaplin. With his iconic bowler hat, toothbrush mustache, and cane, Chaplin's "The Tramp" became one of the most recognizable characters in cinematic history. But Chaplin's brilliance wasn't limited to his on-screen charisma; he was also a director, writer, and producer.

Films like "The Kid" (1921) and "City Lights" (1931) were not just comedic masterpieces but deeply emotional tales that resonated with audiences across socio-economic divides. His ability to blend humor with poignancy, all without uttering a word, showcased the silent era's potential for profound storytelling.

Equally instrumental in shaping silent film comedy was Buster Keaton, the "Great Stone Face." His impassive expression contrasted sharply with Chaplin's emotive style, but this never diminished the impact of his performances. Keaton's films, such as "The General" (1926) and "Sherlock Jr." (1924), were marked by their incredible stunt work and visual gags. Keaton, often risking life and limb, performed his own stunts, resulting in sequences that were as breathtaking as they were hilarious. His innovative use of camera tricks and editing techniques expanded the language of film, demonstrating that cinema wasn't just a recorded stage play but an art form with unique narrative possibilities.

But the silent era wasn't solely the dominion of comedians. Actresses like Mary Pickford, known as "America's Sweetheart," commanded immense audiences. With her golden curls and expressive eyes, Pickford's roles varied from the innocent young girl to the strong-willed heroine, setting the archetype for female protagonists in cinema. She was also a formidable figure behind the scenes, co-founding United Artists alongside Chaplin, Douglas Fairbanks, and D.W. Griffith, granting artists greater control over their productions.

Similarly, stars like Rudolph Valentino became cultural phenomenons. Valentino, with his smoldering on-screen presence in films like "The Sheik" (1921), challenged conventional American notions of masculinity, adding an exotic flavor to the silver screen that left audiences enthralled.

As the industry burgeoned, so did its locations. Films began to capture the vast American landscape, from bustling urban centers to expansive deserts. The epic "Wings" (1927), a war film centered around fighter pilots during World War I, displayed a grandeur and scale previously unimagined, proving that silent films could convey narratives as complex and sweeping as any novel or stage play.

The silent era, while devoid of spoken word, was replete with artistic expression. Through light and shadow, exaggerated gesture, and the evocative power of music, filmmakers of this epoch communicated emotions and stories that transcended language barriers. They didn't need words. Their artistry spoke volumes, setting the stage for cinematic storytelling's endless possibilities.

The silent film era, with its distinct visual storytelling, had established a powerful language of cinema. Still, as the 1920s neared its end, an evolution was brewing that would irrevocably alter the trajectory of filmmaking: the advent of sound. This seismic shift was not just about adding dialogue or music but transforming the very essence of the cinematic experience.

It was a tumultuous journey from conception to reality for sound in cinema. Early attempts at synchronizing phonograph recordings with films were clunky and lacked the finesse required for a truly immersive experience. Technical challenges, such as synchronizing sound with action and amplifying it for a theater audience, seemed insurmountable. But as is often the case with revolutionary ideas, where there's a will, technology finds a way.

The solution lay in the Vitaphone system, developed by Bell Telephone Laboratories and Western Electric, which recorded sound directly onto film. This marked a significant advancement from previous methods and opened the door for filmmakers to experiment with sound-enhanced productions.

Enter "The Jazz Singer" in 1927. Directed by Alan Crosland and featuring Al Jolson, this film wasn't the first to use synchronized sound, but its commercial and cultural impact sent shockwaves through the industry. As Jolson uttered the iconic words, "Wait a minute, wait a minute. You ain't heard nothin' yet!" the future of cinema became evident. It was a moment of sheer magic - characters on screen were no longer just moving figures but entities with voices, capable of singing, crying, and engaging directly with the audience.

The success of "The Jazz Singer" ushered in a frenzy of activity. Studios scrambled to retrofit theaters with sound equipment, and producers sought out actors with stage experience, valuing clear enunciation and vocal charisma. Silent film stars faced the intimidating challenge of adapting to this new format. For some, their distinct voices, which didn't match their on-screen personas, proved to be a career-ending hurdle. For others, it was a golden opportunity to showcase their talents anew.

However, the transition wasn't just a bed of roses. Many purists believed that the incorporation of sound would destroy the artistry of cinema. Charlie Chaplin, a titan of the silent era, was a vocal critic, fearing that the charm and universality of silent films would be lost amidst the clamor of talkies. But as ticket sales for sound films skyrocketed and silent films began to wane in popularity, it became clear that the audience had spoken. They were enchanted by the allure of talkies.

Beyond mere dialogue, the introduction of sound revolutionized other cinematic elements. Film scores became integral to the movie-going experience, guiding emotions and elevating pivotal scenes. Sound effects added layers of realism, immersing audiences further into fictional worlds.

In the wake of "The Jazz Singer," films like "Lights of New York" and "Steamboat Willie," the latter introducing the world to Mickey Mouse, solidified sound's position in cinema. By the early 1930s, the silent film era had receded into the annals of history, and talkies were in full swing, setting the stage for new genres, stars, and storytelling techniques.

Though some mourned the poetic elegance of silent cinema, the talkies' arrival was more than just technological progress; it was a reflection of society's aspirations, desires, and insatiable appetite for innovation. The silent era had set the stage, but with the talkies, cinema found its voice, and it was a voice that resonated deeply, capturing the pulse and rhythm of a changing world.

The rise of talkies did not solely redefine cinematic storytelling; it also heralded the ascent of colossal film studios, institutions that would not only churn out films but dictate the rhythms of Hollywood's heartbeat for decades to come. These film factories, with their assembly-line precision and grandiose visions, sculpted the cinematic landscape and solidified Hollywood's position as the film capital of the world.

Metro-Goldwyn-Mayer, more popularly known as MGM, boasted that they had "more stars than there are in heaven." This wasn't mere hyperbole. The studio, formed in 1924 by the merger of Metro Pictures, Goldwyn Pictures, and Louis B. Mayer Productions, became synonymous with glamour and opulence. Under the discerning eyes of Mayer and Irving Thalberg, the studio produced some of the most unforgettable films of the era, from "Grand Hotel" to "The Wizard of Oz." Their iconic roaring lion logo became a stamp of quality, a promise of cinematic excellence to audiences worldwide.

Just as influential in shaping Hollywood's narrative was Warner Bros. Founded by four Warner brothers—Harry, Albert, Sam, and Jack—in 1923, the studio soon garnered a reputation for its hard-hitting, socially conscious films. Warner Bros. was instrumental in the early adoption of sound in films, with "The Jazz Singer" serving as a testament to their foresight and innovation. Their commitment to realism and tackling socio-political issues set them apart, producing groundbreaking films such as "I Am a Fugitive from a Chain Gang" and "The Public Enemy."

Then there was Paramount Pictures, a studio that predates both MGM and Warner Bros. Founded in 1912, Paramount became a powerhouse in its own right under the guidance of Adolph Zukor. He envisioned films as a form of prestige entertainment and was one of the pioneers of the "star system," luring in top talents with lucrative contracts. The Paramount roster boasted names like Rudolph Valentino, Mae West, and Gary Cooper, and the studio's legacy is peppered with classics such as

"Sunset Boulevard" and "Double Indemnity."

These studios, among others, were part of a vertically integrated system that controlled every stage of a film's life cycle, from production to distribution to exhibition. This was the era of the "studio system." Actors, directors, writers, and producers were often under long-term contracts, with studios exerting significant control over their careers. This structure was both a blessing and a curse. While it ensured a consistent output of films and reduced financial risks for the studios, it also limited creative freedoms and often typecast actors into specific roles.

The implications of the studio system on filmmaking were manifold. The tight schedules and standardized production methods led to a remarkable efficiency. Some studios released a new film every week! Moreover, the in-house roster of talent, both in front of and behind the camera, allowed for a cohesive vision and branding for each studio. MGM films were grand and star-studded, Warner Bros. often gritty and socially relevant, while Paramount prided itself on sophistication and innovation.

However, the system wasn't without its detractors. Some artists bristled against the control exerted by studio moguls, yearning for greater creative autonomy. This push and pull between commercial considerations and artistic aspirations would lay the groundwork for various movements and shifts in Hollywood's history.

The iconic studios of Hollywood's Golden Age did more than produce films. They crafted dreams, wove narratives, and constructed the very mythology of cinema. In their stories, audiences found escapism, reflection, and at times, a redefinition of their own worldviews. Hollywood wasn't just a place; it was an idea, a vision brought to life by these behemoth studios that dared to dream in Technicolor.

The allure of Hollywood was not just its shimmering facades or sprawling sets; it was the magnetic pull of its stars. The very fabric of cinema, its romance and spectacle, were embodied by these larger-than-life figures who graced the silver screen. The "star system," a meticulously crafted machinery, elevated actors to mythic proportions, creating personas that often eclipsed their real identities. In this world of orchestrated glamour, a few names shone especially bright, etching their legacies in the annals of cinematic history.

Clark Gable, with his dashing looks and trademark mustache, was rightfully dubbed the "King of Hollywood." His on-screen charisma was undeniable, but it was his role as Rhett Butler in "Gone with the Wind" that forever cemented his status as an icon. Gable's portrayal of the roguish yet tender-hearted Butler showcased his unparalleled ability to balance strength with vulnerability. Off-screen, his life was marked by personal tragedies and highs and lows, but through it all, he remained the epitome of Hollywood masculinity, a symbol of charm and grace in the face of adversity.

In contrast to Gable's debonair image, Joan Crawford's legacy was built on her unwavering determination and versatility. Starting her career as a flapper in silent films, Crawford's ability to evolve with the changing tides of Hollywood was remarkable. Whether it was the ambitious working girl in "Mildred Pierce" or the twisted matriarch in "Whatever Happened to Baby Jane?", Crawford's chameleonic skills showcased her range and depth. Her off-screen life was riddled with rumors, scandals, and a fierce determination to remain at the top, which she did, for over four decades, a testament to her indomitable spirit.

Then there was Bette Davis, a force to be reckoned with, both on and off the screen. Those piercing eyes and sharp features gave life to some of the most powerful female characters in Hollywood. Films like "All About Eve" and "Jezebel" were testimonies to Davis's unparalleled ability to portray complex, often flawed women with authenticity. Known for her quick wit and uncompromising attitude, Davis was not just an actress; she was an advocate for artists' rights, often clashing with studio heads for fairer contracts and better roles. Her feuds, especially with Joan Crawford, became the stuff of legends, but beyond the headlines, Bette Davis's enduring legacy was her unwavering commitment to her craft.

The star system, orchestrated by the big studios, was not just about finding talent; it was about creating legends. This involved molding their public images, dictating their film roles, and sometimes even their personal lives. Stories of studios arranging publicity dates, altering physical appearances, and even suppressing scandals were rife. But in this controlled chaos, stars like Gable, Crawford, and Davis found ways to shine, to break molds, and to etch their unique imprints.

The intoxicating blend of their on-screen personas, combined with the carefully curated stories of their off-screen lives, made them more than mere actors. They were icons, demigods in the pantheon of cinema. Their lives were tales of passion, ambition, heartbreaks, and triumphs, much like the characters they portrayed. And while the reels of their films might fade, their legacies, illuminated by the glint of starlight, would endure, forever

casting long, inspiring shadows
on the boulevards of
Hollywood.

The roaring twenties ushered in an era of decadence, and as the world twirled in the euphoria of jazz and speakeasies, Hollywood, too, swayed to its own rhythm. The influence of cinema stretched beyond celluloid tales; it weaved its way into the fabric of daily life. And nowhere was this more evident than in the realm of fashion. Hollywood became not just a dream factory but also a trendsetter, its style dictums echoing in the corridors of Parisian couture houses and reverberating in the bustling markets of New York.

In this sartorial symphony, one name stood out like a soaring crescendo: Edith Head. With her signature round glasses and poised demeanor, she was more than a costume designer; she was a visionaire. Her understanding of the human form, combined with her innate ability to marry character essence with fabric, made her an indomitable force in Hollywood fashion. Head's creations for stars like Audrey Hepburn in "Roman Holiday" and Grace Kelly in "Rear Window" weren't just outfits; they were statements, telling tales more eloquent than dialogues ever could. For her, fashion wasn't just about aesthetics; it was about identity, an unspoken dialogue between the character and the audience.

But Edith Head's genius wasn't an isolated phenomenon. Hollywood was a melting pot of sartorial innovation. Take, for instance, the iconic white halter dress worn by Marilyn Monroe in "The Seven Year Itch". That billowing silhouette against the urban backdrop wasn't just a scene; it was a fashion moment, signaling the uninhibited spirit of a post-war generation. The genius behind this iconic look was William Travilla, a name synonymous with crafting Monroe's most memorable on-screen looks.

As these designers spun magic with their needles and threads, Hollywood became the global epicenter of style. The screen sirens of this era weren't just actors; they were fashion icons. People emulated their hairstyles, their makeup, and, most importantly, their attire. The sharp suits donned by Humphrey Bogart, the sultry gowns of Rita Hayworth, and the sophisticated elegance of Katharine Hepburn were more than just wardrobe choices; they were cultural signifiers, markers of an era defined by its style.

But Hollywood's influence wasn't limited to haute couture or upscale boutiques. It trickled down to department stores and everyday wardrobes. Women yearned for the pencil skirts and tailored blouses sported by their favorite actresses, while men tilted their hats just so, emulating the debonair charm of silver screen heartthrobs. Hairstyles, accessories, even lipstick shades–every nuanced detail was replicated, reinterpreted, and reintegrated into global fashion.

And as cinema evolved, so did its fashion narrative. The war years saw a shift towards austerity, with fabric rationing influencing designs. But even in these times, Hollywood found ways to innovate, making do with less yet creating iconic wartime looks that blended practicality with style.

In essence, Hollywood's Golden Age was more than a cinematic renaissance; it was a fashion revolution. Every frame, every costume, was a canvas, painted with the hues of imagination and innovation. And as the lights dimmed and the projector whirred to life, audiences were treated to not just tales of love and drama but also a visual feast, a sartorial spectacle that would influence generations of fashionistas the world over.

I n the midst of glitter and glamour, where stories spun wild and characters came alive, there was an undercurrent of restriction, a whisper of control. Hollywood, with all its audacity and creativity, wasn't free from the bounds of societal expectations. The Hays Code, officially the Motion Picture Production Code, became the invisible hand that guided, and at times, stifled the filmmakers of the Golden Age.

In the late 1920s and early 1930s, Hollywood films began to explore daring themes, reflecting the societal upheavals and the newfound freedom of the Jazz Age. Risqué dances, hints of homosexuality, and insinuations of illicit relationships peppered the screens. But as the movies became bolder, so did the voices against them. Religious groups, politicians, and concerned citizens rallied against what they saw as a descent into immorality.

Enter Will H. Hays, the figure appointed to sanitize Hollywood. As the president of the Motion Picture Producers and Distributors of America (MPPDA), Hays was tasked with the monumental job of ensuring that films projected a wholesome image, aligning with traditional values. By 1934, with the input of Catholic clergymen Martin Quigley and Daniel A. Lord, the Hays Code was adopted industry-wide.

The code was comprehensive, and its edicts were clear. Adultery, explicit violence, and miscegenation were forbidden.

Scenes of passion were to be subdued, and criminal activities could not be portrayed in a manner that would elicit sympathy. Even the duration of on-screen kisses was regulated. Beyond the evident, the code had subtle implications, too. Heroes and villains were more distinctly demarcated, with evil consistently meeting its comeuppance.

But with restriction came innovation. Filmmakers, ever the creative lot, found ways around the stringent regulations. They mastered the art of insinuation, letting shadows tell tales and using clever dialogues to hint at the forbidden. The constraints of the Hays Code, inadvertently, led to some of the most ingenious moments in cinematic storytelling.

Film noir, a genre characterized by its moody aesthetics and morally ambiguous characters, thrived in this environment. The dark alleys and the play of light and shadow became metaphors for the gray areas of morality. Similarly, comedies employed double entendres, allowing adult audiences to read between the lines while ensuring the content remained palatable for the censors.

Yet, for all its clever circumventions, the Hays Code did take a toll on storytelling. Diverse narratives, especially those dealing with LGBTQ+

themes, were pushed underground. The rich tapestry of human experience was, at times, reduced to monochrome, with complexities brushed under the carpet in favor of a more 'wholesome' narrative.

The reign of the Hays Code continued until the 1960s, when societal norms began to shift once more. With the advent of New Hollywood and a renewed push for creative freedom, the code was replaced by the modern film rating system. But its legacy, both in terms of the challenges it posed and the creativity it inadvertently spurred, remains etched in the annals of Hollywood history.

In retrospect, the Hays Code serves as a reflection of its time: an era grappling with rapid societal changes, trying to balance artistic freedom with perceived morality. The stories from this period, both on-screen and behind the scenes, are a testament to the human spirit's resilience and the undying drive to tell tales, even in the face of adversity.

The lush palm trees swayed in the Californian breeze, seemingly whispering secrets of the glitz and allure of Hollywood. But, like any realm of glamour and opulence,

Hollywood's shimmering facade often concealed tumultuous tales of passion, intrigue, and scandal. As the film reels spun stories of dreamy romances and valorous tales, off-screen narratives were just as compelling and, at times, far more tragic.

Hollywood's elite lived life under the relentless gaze of the spotlight. Every dalliance, every misstep was fodder for the burgeoning tabloid industry. The paparazzi, with their flashbulbs perpetually at the ready, lurked in every shadowed corner, hungry for a scoop.

One of the most sensational tales from this era was that of Clara Bow, the vivacious "It" girl.

Her magnetic screen presence and unabashed sexuality made her a sensation, but her off-screen life was punctuated by controversy. Rumors swirled about her relationships, wild parties, and alleged escapades, many of them sensationalized or entirely fabricated by tabloids eager for a salacious headline. The pressures of fame and relentless scrutiny, compounded by personal struggles, led to her premature retirement from the silver screen.

But Bow's tale wasn't an isolated one. Roscoe "Fatty" Arbuckle, a silent film star, found himself embroiled in a scandal that would forever tarnish his legacy. Accused of causing the death of actress Virginia Rappe, Arbuckle faced three trials, with the media painting him as a monster. Although he was eventually acquitted, his career never fully recovered, a testament to the tabloid's power in shaping public perception.

The love affairs of the Hollywood elite also kept the rumor mills churning. The passionate and tumultuous relationship between Elizabeth Taylor and Richard Burton was the stuff of legends, their every move chronicled and dissected. Similarly, the whirlwind romance of Frank Sinatra and Ava Gardner was splashed across front pages, their love story as captivating as any cinematic tale.

However, not all scandals were born from personal indiscretions. Hollywood's ties with the political landscape were under constant scrutiny, especially during the McCarthy era. Accusations of Communist ties led to the infamous Hollywood blacklist, where artists, writers, and actors were shunned, their careers derailed by mere suspicion.

Yet, amidst the scandal and intrigue, the essence of Hollywood's Golden Age remained untarnished. For every salacious headline, there were countless tales of camaraderie, passion for the craft, and a collective drive to create magic on screen. The scandals, while defining moments in many stars' lives, were mere footnotes in the grand narrative of Hollywood, a realm where reality often blended seamlessly with fiction.

The Golden Age was a time of paradoxes. The same era that witnessed unparalleled artistic achievements also grappled with the complexities of fame, the consequences of living life in the public eye, and the challenges of navigating a world where truth was often stranger than fiction.

The silver screen shimmered with the luminance of its stars. Icons like Audrey Hepburn, Humphrey Bogart, and Marilyn Monroe became synonymous with the glamour of Hollywood. But behind every impeccable costume, each flawless set, and all timeless cinematic moments were legions of dedicated professionals, the unsung heroes of Hollywood.

The studio era was a meticulously orchestrated machine. For each movie that made it to the big screen, countless hours of labor, artistry, and collaboration went on behind the scenes. Without the magic touch of these dedicated professionals, the Golden Age of Hollywood might have been a far less lustrous affair.

In the labyrinthine studios, set designers and builders toiled endlessly. They crafted entire worlds within the confines of sound stages, from the opulent palaces of historical epics to the dimly lit streets of film noir. Their craft was a blend of art and architecture, bringing to life the visions of directors and screenwriters.

The art of cinematography was as crucial as the script or the performances. Cinematographers like Gregg Toland, with his deep focus technique in "Citizen Kane," and James Wong Howe, known for his pioneering use of lighting, transformed the way stories were visualized. Their lenses captured more than scenes; they captured moods, emotions, and the very essence of narratives.

Sound engineers, too, played a pivotal role. With the advent of talkies, synchronizing sound became an intricate ballet of precision. Ambient sounds, dialogues, and musical scores were woven together to create a seamless auditory experience. Films like "Singin' in the Rain" showcased not just the front-of-camera talent, but also the meticulous soundscapes curated behind the scenes.

Makeup and costume departments were bustling hubs of creativity. The visage of the stars, their iconic looks and styles, were often the handiwork of makeup artists who understood the nuances of lighting and film. Jack Pierce's transformative makeup design for Boris Karloff in "Frankenstein" remains iconic. Costumers, such as the aforementioned Edith Head, tailored not just clothes but character personas, understanding the symbiotic relationship between attire and performance.

And then there were the screenwriters, often the most overlooked of Hollywood's maestros. Their pens birthed dialogues that became a part of the cultural lexicon, plots that resonated across generations, and characters that became immortal. Writers like Billy Wilder, Frances Marion, and

Dalton Trumbo (before his blacklisting) were the keystones of the filmic universe.

Yet, for all their indispensable contributions, many of these craftsmen and women remained in the shadows, eclipsed by the wattage of the stars they elevated. Hollywood's Golden Age was not just the age of cinematic icons; it was the era of relentless dedication, of countless unsung heroes who, with their expertise and passion, built the very foundations of the cinematic world we cherish. Their legacies, though less celebrated, are embedded in every frame, every note, and every line of the classics we hold dear.

The Golden Age of Hollywood was characterized by its rich diversity in storytelling. Though often seen through a nostalgic lens as an era of glamour and romance, the films of this time spanned a myriad of genres, each contributing to the rich tapestry of cinematic history. These genres not only entertained but reflected the zeitgeist of their times, capturing the hopes, fears, dreams, and realities of the society they served.

The Musical was a genre that truly encapsulated the spirit of escapism. In a world reeling from economic depression and on the brink of global conflict, films like "Top Hat" and "Meet Me in St. Louis" offered audiences a respite from their daily woes, transporting them into a world of song, dance, and Technicolor dreams. Musicals celebrated life, love, and the simple joys, creating a harmonious universe where conflicts were resolved with a tap dance or a soulful ballad.

Contrasting the light-hearted musicals were the Film Noirs. These were tales from the underbelly of urban life, where the line between right and wrong was often blurred. Shadows played a vital role in this genre, both literally and metaphorically. Films like "Double Indemnity" and "The Maltese Falcon" explored themes of crime, passion, and betrayal, with protagonists who were as flawed as they were charismatic. Film Noir didn't just tell stories; it delved into the human psyche, revealing the grey shades that lurk within.

Westerns, on the other hand, painted a picture of a bygone era, a time of pioneers and outlaws, of vast landscapes and frontier justice. Movies like "Stagecoach" and "High Noon" weren't just tales of cowboys and Indians; they were reflections on morality, honor, and the eternal battle between civilization and wilderness. The Western genre was a canvas on which filmmakers painted their perceptions of American history, mythology, and identity.

Romantic dramas like "Casablanca" and "Gone with the Wind" wove tales of love, loss, and longing against the backdrop of war and societal upheavals. These films spoke of personal sacrifices, the choices one makes in the face of adversity, and the enduring nature of love.

Then there were the comedies. Masters like Charlie Chaplin and the Marx Brothers used humor as a lens to comment on society, politics, and human nature. Their films, while uproariously funny, often carried deeper messages about class divides, war, and the human condition.

Horror films, spearheaded by studios like Universal, brought to life the monsters of lore and literature. "Dracula", "Frankenstein", and "The Mummy" were more than just tales of the supernatural; they delved into themes of otherness, man's relationship with nature, and the consequences of playing God.

As varied as these genres were, they all had one thing in common: they held up a mirror to society. Through their stories, characters, and settings, they explored the human condition in all its complexities. The Golden Age of Hollywood was not just golden because of its stars or its box office successes, but because of its unparalleled ability to tell stories that resonated, that made audiences laugh and cry, hope and dream.

T he early days of Hollywood were monochromatic. Film reels spun tales in gradients of gray, painting narratives with shadows and light. But as the industry evolved, so did its palette. The arrival of Technicolor brought with it a burst of vibrancy that forever transformed the cinematic landscape.

The Technicolor process was, in essence, a revolution. Before its inception, attempts at color in cinema were rudimentary, often involving hand-coloring individual frames or using two-color processes that didn't capture the full spectrum of hues. Technicolor's three-strip process changed all that. By recording the red, green, and blue components of a scene separately and then combining them, the process could produce films with an almost complete spectrum of colors.

The first films to employ this technique were met with a sense of wonderment. Audiences were mesmerized by the lush landscapes, the intricate costumes, and the lifelike reproduction of reality. When "Becky Sharp" premiered in 1935 as the first feature film in full Technicolor, it heralded a new era. The film, though modest in its narrative ambitions, showcased the sheer visual possibilities of this new technology.

But with new opportunities came new challenges. Directors, cinematographers, and production designers had to relearn their crafts. The Technicolor process was more cumbersome than black and white filming, requiring brighter lights and producing more heat on set. Makeup and costume departments had to adapt to how colors appeared on film. Reds and greens, for example, appeared vastly different under Technicolor's process than in reality.

However, the results were nothing short of magical. "The Adventures of Robin Hood" showcased vibrant forests and Errol Flynn's dashing red attire, making it a visual feast. "Gone with the Wind" painted its historical epic with a lavish brush, from the burning of Atlanta to the iconic sunset backdrops.

But Technicolor wasn't just about spectacle; it was a storytelling tool. Filmmakers realized that color could convey emotions, set tones, and symbolize themes. The yellow brick road and the emerald city in "The Wizard of Oz" weren't just aesthetic choices; they were narrative ones, drawing audiences into a world where dreams could come true.

Musicals, with their grand set-pieces, particularly benefited from this chromatic transformation. The underwater sequence in "An American in Paris" or the barn-raising scene in "Seven Brides for Seven Brothers" showcased Technicolor's ability to elevate sequences to new visual heights.

However, as with all innovations, Technicolor had its detractors. Some believed that color detracted from the essence of storytelling, making films more about spectacle than narrative. But as history would prove, Technicolor was not a mere gimmick. It was a tool, another brush in a filmmaker's kit, allowing them to paint stories in hues previously unimaginable.

By the 1960s, as other color processes became more efficient and cost-effective, Technicolor's dominance waned. Yet its impact was indelible. The Golden Age of

Hollywood, with its tales of love, adventure, and dreams, became all the more enchanting, painted in the myriad shades of Technicolor's rainbow.

I n the early days of Hollywood, the production process was an assembly line. Scripts were crafted by committees of writers, films were overseen by studio moguls, and directors, though respected, often worked within strict confines, executing the vision set out by their studio masters. But as the Golden Age matured, a shift began to take place. Some directors started to exert more control, stamping their unique signatures onto their films. This heralded the rise of the auteur.

The term "auteur" is French for "author." In the context of cinema, it suggests that a director, despite collaborating with hundreds or even thousands of people, can be the primary 'author' or 'voice' of a film. The idea was that just as one can identify a novel by its author, one should be able to identify a film by its director.

This wasn't an instantaneous transformation. It was a slow, evolving process nurtured by directors who dared to push boundaries and challenge the status quo. Alfred Hitchcock, for instance, wasn't just a director; he was a brand. His films, from "Rear Window" to "Psycho," bore unmistakable hallmarks: suspenseful plots, iconic camera angles, and intricate character studies. The name 'Hitchcock' became synonymous with a certain kind of thriller, and audiences flocked to theaters not just for the stars or the story, but for the man behind the camera.

Orson Welles, another towering figure of this movement, exploded onto the scene with

"Citizen Kane." The film, with its innovative narrative structure, deep focus cinematography, and nuanced character study, showcased what an auteur could accomplish when given free rein. Though the film faced challenges upon release, in hindsight, it stands as a testament to Welles' genius and the power of a singular vision.

John Ford, with his sweeping Westerns, created a world that was uniquely his. His films, like "The Searchers" and "Stagecoach," weren't just tales of cowboys and open plains; they were meditations on America, its history, and its myths. The landscapes in a Ford film weren't mere backdrops; they were characters, silent witnesses to the unfolding human drama.

While these auteurs were crafting their masterpieces, they were often at odds with studios, battling for control and creative freedom. This tension, between commercial imperatives and artistic aspirations, defined much of the era. Studios, wary of investing vast sums without assurance, often balked at the unconventional ideas of these directors. Yet, time and again, these auteurs proved that their visions, though distinct and sometimes challenging, resonated deeply with audiences.

The rise of the auteur was not just a shift in production

dynamics; it was a redefinition of cinema itself. Films were no longer just entertainment products; they were works of art, expressions of individual creativity, and mirrors to the souls of their creators.

By the end of the Golden Age, as the studio system began its decline and the industry moved towards a new paradigm, the auteur movement had firmly taken root. Directors were no longer just craftsmen; they were artists, storytellers, and visionaries, pushing cinema into new, uncharted territories.

The rise of Hollywood musicals was a celebration of life, color, and rhythm. As the world grappled with the challenges of the Great Depression, war, and sociopolitical upheaval, the silver screen provided an escape —a haven where dreams could come true, if only for a couple of hours.

Musicals of the Golden Age were grand spectacles. Studios would pour enormous resources into these productions, resulting in breathtaking dance numbers, imaginative sets, and unforgettable songs. The vibrant world of Hollywood musicals promised a reality where problems could be danced away, where love always triumphed, and where song was the universal language of the heart.

Fred Astaire and Ginger Rogers were the quintessential dance pair of the 1930s. Their on-screen chemistry was electric, turning films like "Top Hat" and "Swing Time" into instant classics. Astaire, with his impeccable timing and smooth moves, paired with Rogers, graceful and charismatic, showed the world that dance could be an intimate conversation, a romance, and a spectacle all at once.

However, it wasn't just the big numbers that defined these films; it was the emotion behind them. Judy Garland, with her powerful voice and vulnerable presence, gave the world "Over the Rainbow" in "The Wizard of Oz." The song wasn't just about a fantastical world; it was a yearning, a hope for something better beyond the horizon.

The 1950s saw the musical genre reach new heights. MGM's "Singin' in the Rain," though set during the transition from silent films to talkies, was an ode to Hollywood itself. Gene Kelly, with his athletic dance style and contagious enthusiasm, splashed and spun through rain-soaked streets, reminding audiences of the simple joys of life.

Musicals also provided an avenue for cultural exchange. "West Side Story," a modern retelling of Shakespeare's "Romeo and Juliet," used song and dance to explore themes of racial tension and love in a divided New York City. With its poignant songs and electrifying dance sequences, the film captured the heartbreak of young love against a backdrop of societal conflict.

Behind these glorious productions were visionaries like director Vincente Minnelli and choreographer Busby Berkeley. Berkeley, with his kaleidoscopic choreographies, transformed dance into a visual spectacle, using geometric patterns, synchronized movements, and innovative camera angles. Minnelli, on the other hand, had a knack for marrying emotion with aesthetics, turning musicals into emotionally resonant visual feasts.

Yet, like all things, the Golden Age of Hollywood musicals began to wane. By the 1960s, as societal attitudes shifted and filmmaking evolved, the grand musicals of yore started feeling out of place. But their legacy was cemented. They had shown that cinema wasn't just a medium for storytelling; it was a canvas for dreams, hopes, and the unfettered joy of song and dance.

In the Golden Age of Hollywood, women were not merely passive figures on the silver screen; they were dynamic forces, influencing and molding the industry in myriad ways. With charisma, talent, and undeniable presence, the leading ladies of this era were emblematic of the changes happening in society and the evolving perceptions of femininity.

Greta Garbo, with her enigmatic allure, captured audiences with her blend of vulnerability and strength. In films like "Camille" and "Ninotchka," she traversed a range of emotions, showcasing her versatility. Garbo's mystique was so potent that her tagline "Garbo Talks!" was enough to generate immense buzz for her transition from silent to sound films.

Katharine Hepburn, with her sharp wit and independent

spirit, was a breed apart. Refusing to conform to the cookie-cutter image of a starlet, Hepburn wore pants, spoke her mind, and selected roles that defied convention. From her rebellious portrayal in "Bringing Up Baby" to her fierce independence in "The African Queen," Hepburn shattered stereotypes, proving that leading ladies could be both strong and feminine.

Then there was Bette Davis, with her piercing eyes and unyielding determination. Davis was unafraid to take on complex, often unlikable characters, pushing the boundaries of what was expected from female roles. In films like "All About Eve" and

"Jezebel," she showcased the depth and multi-dimensionality of her characters, earning acclaim and cementing her place as one of Hollywood's finest.

Marilyn Monroe, though often typecast as the naive blonde bombshell, brought depth and vulnerability to her roles. Beneath the glitz and glamour, Monroe's performances in films like "Some Like It Hot" and "The Seven Year Itch" hinted at a deeper understanding of the human condition. Her blend of sensuality and innocence made her an icon, symbolizing the complexities of femininity.

But the Golden Age wasn't just about leading ladies in front of the camera; it also saw pioneering women working behind the scenes. Directors like Dorothy Arzner and Ida Lupino carved out spaces in a male-dominated industry, crafting narratives that were sensitive, insightful, and often ahead of their time.

These women, both on and off-screen, navigated a Hollywood that was rife with challenges. From the constraints of the studio system to societal expectations, leading ladies of the era often had to fight for their place under the spotlight. But fight they did, laying the groundwork for future generations of actresses and filmmakers.

As the curtains drew on the Golden Age, the legacy of its leading ladies was undeniable. They had redefined stardom, challenged norms, and left an indelible mark on cinema. Their tales of triumph, heartbreak, resilience, and rebellion continue to resonate, reminding us of the power of the feminine spirit in the world of celluloid.

The leading men of Hollywood's Golden Age were more than just handsome faces on screen; they were embodiments of the changing masculine ideal, reflecting the socio-political shifts and cultural aspirations of the time. These men, with their varied personas, captivated audiences, offering visions of heroism, romance, and the complexities of the male psyche.

Humphrey Bogart, with his rugged charm and distinctive voice, emerged as an unlikely romantic hero. In films like "Casablanca," he portrayed characters with a hardened exterior but a heart of gold. Bogart's characters often grappled with their morals, showcasing the internal conflicts faced by many during tumultuous times. The iconic line, "Here's looking at you, kid," delivered with a mix of pain and longing, encapsulated the essence of his on-screen presence.

Gary Cooper, tall and stoic, embodied the quintessential American hero. His roles in movies such as "High Noon" showcased a man of few words but strong convictions, a figure who would stand up against injustice even when the odds were stacked against him. Cooper's portrayals resonated with an America that was transitioning from the hardships of the Depression to the challenges of World War II, seeking figures of quiet resilience.

James Dean, though his career was tragically short-lived,

became the symbol of youthful rebellion. In "Rebel Without a Cause," he captured the angst and disillusionment of a generation struggling to find its place in a rapidly changing world. His untimely death further solidified his legend, making him an eternal symbol of the restless spirit of youth.

Errol Flynn, with his swashbuckling roles, offered escapism and adventure. His portrayal of Robin Hood showcased a charismatic leader, both rogue and hero, who would defy corrupt authorities for the greater good. Flynn's off-screen life, filled with adventures and controversies, only added to his larger-than-life image.

Cary Grant, suave and sophisticated, brought elegance to the big screen. Whether in romantic comedies like "His Girl Friday" or suspense thrillers by Hitchcock, Grant showcased impeccable comedic timing and a unique ability to bring depth to light-hearted roles. His on-screen charisma was so potent that he remained a leading man for several decades, adapting to the changing tastes of audiences.

Off the screen, many of these actors were involved in the major events and causes of their time. Whether it was supporting the war effort, championing civil rights, or shaping the political discourse, they wielded influence that extended beyond the cinematic realm.

As the Golden Age progressed, the image of the leading man evolved, reflecting the complexities and contradictions of masculinity. They were heroes and anti-heroes, lovers and fighters, symbols of strength, and emblems of vulnerability. Through their performances, they offered glimpses into the many facets of manhood, leaving behind legacies that continue to shape the portrayal of men in cinema.

While the stars of the Golden Age dazzled audiences with their on-screen performances, a cadre of talented individuals worked tirelessly behind the scenes to bring these cinematic experiences to life. Directors, producers, screenwriters, cinematographers, and countless others collaborated in the intricate dance of filmmaking, transforming raw ideas into timeless classics.

Alfred Hitchcock, the "Master of Suspense," was one such luminary. With a meticulous eye for detail and a penchant for psychological thrillers, Hitchcock redefined the boundaries of cinema. His innovative use of camera angles, shadow play, and storytelling techniques in films like "Psycho" and "Rear Window" kept audiences on the edge of their seats, while also inviting them to ponder deeper existential questions.

Orson Welles, though he started as a wunderkind of the radio era, soon became a force to reckon with in Hollywood. His debut film, "Citizen Kane," is often hailed as one of the greatest films ever made. With its deep focus cinematography, nonlinear narrative, and sharp commentary on media magnates, Welles showcased a level of innovation that was decades ahead of its time.

Cecil B. DeMille was the epitome of spectacle. His grand epics, such as "The Ten Commandments" and "Cleopatra," were a testament to his vision of cinema as a larger-than-life experience. DeMille's sets were massive, his stories grandiose, and his ambition boundless, making him one of the most influential directors of the era.

But it wasn't just directors who shaped the Golden Age. Screenwriters like Billy Wilder, who penned classics like "Sunset Boulevard" and "Some Like It Hot," brought wit, humor, and depth to the silver screen. His sharp dialogues and intricate character developments were crucial in elevating films from mere entertainment to profound reflections on society.

Cinematographers, too, played a pivotal role. Gregg Toland's groundbreaking work in "Citizen

Kane," for instance, changed the way stories were visually told. His innovative techniques, from deep focus to low-angle shots, enabled narratives to unfold in more dynamic and layered ways.

The era also saw producers like David O. Selznick, who, with films like "Gone with the Wind," showed that a producer's role wasn't just financial but also creative. Selznick was involved in every aspect of his films, from script revisions to casting, ensuring that the final product matched his vision.

These visionaries, each in their own way, shaped the cinematic landscape of the Golden Age. They experimented, innovated, and took risks, challenging conventions and pushing boundaries. While the stars might have been the faces of the films, these behind-the-scenes maestros were the heart and soul, driving the industry forward and leaving an indelible mark on the annals of cinema.

In the pantheon of Hollywood's Golden Age, musicals occupy a place of reverence. With their delightful blend of song, dance, and narrative, these films offered audiences an escape from the mundanities of life, transporting them to a world where emotions were expressed in melodic harmonies and where love stories unfolded amidst synchronized tap routines.

Gene Kelly's name is synonymous with the musical genre. His athletic dance style and magnetic screen presence came to the fore in films like "Singin' in the Rain." In this timeless classic, Kelly not only showcased his dancing prowess but also his talent as a choreographer, crafting routines that blended ballet, tap, and modern dance. The iconic scene where he dances with unabated joy in pouring rain remains etched in cinematic memory.

Fred Astaire, with his elegant style and impeccable timing, was another stalwart of musicals. Films like "Top Hat" and "Swing Time" showcased his incredible chemistry with Ginger Rogers. Together, they glided across the screen, making complex routines look effortless. Astaire's influence wasn't limited to his dance; he was also instrumental in ensuring that dance sequences were shot in long takes, allowing audiences to fully appreciate the choreography.

But it wasn't just individual performances that defined this era's musicals. Productions like

"The Sound of Music," with its memorable soundtrack and breathtaking Alpine landscapes, showcased the genre's ability to combine storytelling with musical brilliance. Julie Andrews' portrayal of Maria, a vivacious nun turned governess, struck a chord with audiences, making the film a perennial favorite.

Then there was "West Side Story," a modern retelling of Romeo and Juliet set against the backdrop of New York's gang wars. With its pulsating dance numbers and poignant songs, the film tackled themes of love, prejudice, and cultural conflict, showcasing the genre's capacity to deal with serious issues while still providing entertainment.

Behind these musicals were composers and lyricists whose contributions were immeasurable. Rodgers and Hammerstein, George and Ira Gershwin, Irving Berlin - these were just some of the luminaries who crafted unforgettable tunes that became part of the cultural lexicon. Songs like "Somewhere Over the Rainbow" from "The Wizard of Oz" or "As Time Goes By" from "Casablanca," while not from traditional musicals, demonstrated the era's penchant for memorable melodies.

The Golden Age musicals were more than mere entertainment; they were cultural phenomena. They reflected society's joys, sorrows, hopes, and dreams, all set to a melodious soundtrack. As the final notes of this era faded and cinema evolved, the legacy of these musicals remained, reminding us of a time when life's emotions were best expressed through song and dance.

As the 1950s drew to a close, Hollywood's Golden Age began to dim, giving way to a new era of filmmaking. The studio system, which had been the backbone of

Hollywood's production for decades, began to crumble. New technologies, the advent of television, changing audience tastes, and societal shifts marked the beginning of significant transformations in the cinematic landscape.

The rise of television posed a direct threat to the movie industry. The convenience of entertainment in the living room meant fewer people venturing out to the theaters. Hollywood tried to counter this with innovations like CinemaScope, offering widescreen spectacles that couldn't be replicated on small TV screens. Epics like "Ben-Hur" and "Spartacus" sought to draw audiences with their grandeur.

Independent filmmakers began to emerge, challenging the established norms and offering alternative narratives. Directors like Stanley Kubrick, John Cassavetes, and later, the pioneers of New Hollywood like Francis Ford Coppola and Martin Scorsese, ushered in a fresh perspective, moving away from the polished aesthetics of the Golden Age to more raw and realistic portrayals.

Yet, even as this epoch ended, its influence persisted. The Golden Age had laid the groundwork for everything that followed in cinema. The storytelling techniques, character archetypes, and even specific film genres established during this time continued to inform and inspire filmmakers.

The stars of the Golden Age, too, left an indelible mark. Their legacies, whether through memorable roles or off-screen contributions, continued to influence new generations of actors. The charisma of a Clark Gable or the nuanced performance of a Bette Davis became benchmarks for future talents.

But perhaps the most significant contribution of the Golden Age was its encapsulation of a certain zeitgeist. These films captured the hopes, dreams, fears, and aspirations of a generation. They offered escape during the Great Depression, buoyed spirits during the war, and reflected the evolving societal norms in the post-war years.

In today's age, where streaming has revolutionized how we consume content, and films from across the world are at our fingertips, the classics of the Golden Age still hold a special place. They're not just nostalgic relics but masterpieces that resonate with timeless themes. They remind us of a period of unparalleled creativity and innovation in cinema.

And so, while the curtains may have drawn on Hollywood's Golden Age, its glow remains undiminished. The era stands as a testament to the power of cinema – its ability to entertain, inspire, challenge, and most importantly, to endure. The end of this age wasn't so much a conclusion as it was a transition, paving the way for new stories, new voices, and new horizons in the world of filmmaking.

www.ingramcontent.com/pod-product-compliance
Lightning Source LLC
Chambersburg PA
CBHW030013190526
45157CB00016B/2691